# BULLYPROOF
## Unleash the Hero Inside Your Kid

# BULLYPROOF
## Unleash the Hero Inside Your Kid
## VOLUME 3

### CONTRIBUTING AUTHORS:
JESSE BERNAL

VINCENT-MARCO DUCHETTA

DANIEL GRYCZKA

TODD HARRIS

JAKE MIESNER

JOSE MONTERO

JEREMY ROADRUCK

BRIAN SEETGE

### EDITORS:
MICHAEL CUDDYER

ALEX CHANGHO

# BULLYPROOF
## Unleash the Hero Inside Your Kid
## Volume 3

# DEDICATION

To each and every man, woman, boy and girl who has
shown kindness to another person, has helped someone
who was feeling down, or has empowered another person
to be confident and strong: thank you.

# TABLE OF CONTENTS

# FOREWORD

*By Alice Geiss, M. Ed.; NBCT*

I am very honored that Alex has asked me to write the foreword

for Volume 3 of the BULLYPROOF Series. Alex and I have known

each other for over 13 years and we share the same vision that in

the journey of teaching our children about bully prevention we

need to instill the need of self-empowerment. As much as we want

the bully behaviors to stop, the strength and power needs to shine

through from the person receiving the bullying behavior.

So how do we go about getting this done? As a professional school

counselor for the past 25 years the focus of my counseling and guidance has been to teach and encourage skills of communication; self-appreciation; conflict resolution; tolerance; and empathy for others. With repeated opportunities to practice these skills, a level of comfort will develop, which in turn will create a sense of empowerment. When speaking with my students I tell them that no matter if the behavior they are experiencing from someone else is a bullying behavior, a rude behavior and/or teasing behavior it is essential that they seek out help from a caring adult. Too often our children do not tell the adults, in their lives, what is happening and in turn the bullying behaviors continue.

Over the last 5 to 10 years I have observed an increase of the words "bully" and "bullying" to be used incorrectly. It has become quite easy to label any undesired behavior that we experience as bullying. No doubt, bullying is a serious issue that too many students are experiencing daily and these true bullying behaviors need to be taken care of immediately and effectively.
I believe that we also need to teach the children's significant others the correct meaning of bullying. Our children look up to us

and will define bullying the way their adult role models are defining bullying. There needs to be an increased understanding that bullying is correctly described as a repeated unwanted behavior that has the intention of gaining power over someone and/or to hurt some physically and/or emotionally.

My hope is that the BULLYPROOF Series becomes somewhat like a handbook for parents to use to help them help and encourage their children to become empowered and strong so that they will not be perceived as a victim and be bullyproof.

Alice Geiss completed her master in school counseling at the University of North Carolina at Charlotte in 1987 and earned National Board Certification in School Counseling through the National Board for Professional Teaching Standards in 2004 and 2014. Alice currently works as a school counselor at an elementary school in the Wake County Public School System.

# INTRODUCTION:
# GOD SAID LOVE YOUR ENEMY

## BY ALEX CHANGHO
## APEX, NORTH CAROLINA

A couple of months before the publication of this third Volume of

*BULLYPROOF: Unleash the Hero Inside Your Kid*, there was one of

those "awareness campaigns" on Facebook.  You know, the ones

that say "To combat the negativity on Facebook, I'm going to flood

my feed with comic book super heroes, and if you comment, I'll tell

you which one to post too!"

Of course, it's a nice sentiment, and lots of people posted their favorite super hero comic book characters.

Of course, I, being the cheeky type, took one look at that and rolled my eyes. And then, I stopped. I thought for a moment, and decided to play along... just differently.

And so grabbed my phone, picked a cool picture, and used the Word Swag App on my iPhone, and made this:

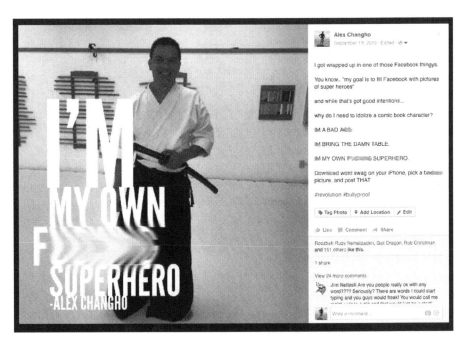

Needless to say, it caused a bit of a stir.  On one hand, there were a small but vocal number of people who expressed their dismay at the use of profanity in such a way.

What struck me even more powerfully, however, was the outpouring of support for this kind of attitude: how wonderful it was that we can be our own heroes.

In Volume 1 of *BULLYPROOF*, which was released only a few months ago before this Volume but seems oh so long ago, I told the story of how Luke Skywalker was my super hero growing up— that is, until I learned to have the confidence to be my own superhero.

The question remains, however, how one finds true confidence.

Most of the contributing authors to BULLYPROOF are, like me, veteran martial artists.  We've been joined by a chiropractor, a medical doctor, and a life coach.  But regardless of the background, we all promote the individual empowerment of a child, teen, or adult.

Ultimately, that comes down to a very simple, yet challenging, idea: that of self-love, and of acceptance.

It is when a child, teen, man or woman can finally, at their core, be in a state of total, unconditional self-acceptance, can one find love and confidence. This is not to say that one will settle, and choose not to grow; on the contrary, real growth can only come from understanding exactly where one starts. And that is found through acceptance of where you are today, without judgment.

It is when a person loves themself and accepts themself that they become impervious to the external forces that seek to bully them, hurt them, or intimidate them. Again, bullying may never go away, but the person who is bullyproof isn't affected by their efforts.

As we continue our quest to bullyproof that world, one child at a time, we must always remember the first and most vital step—

although it may, in many cases, be the most difficult.  We must be the examples of bullyproof to those we raise, teach, and support. We must accept ourselves for who we are, love ourselves, so that our charges can do the same for themselves.

As we delve into the experiences of these eight authors, I finish with one more social media meme, which featured the following quotation:

*"And God said 'Love your enemy'*

*so I obeyed him and loved myself."*

*–Khalil Gibran.*

Be bullyproof.  Love yourself.

Alex Changho is a lifestyle and business coach. With almost two decades of experience leading and motivating others, and running a business, he helps business owners integrate their life's mission and career with their personal side of their life.

An accomplished speaker and presenter, Alex is a Master NLP Practitioner and Trainer, Senior Leader with Anthony Robbins, and Master Strengths Coach.

Alex lives in North Carolina with his cat Bert.

For more information, visit www.alexchangho.com.

# CHAPTER 1: STRATEGIES TO COMBAT BULLYING

## BY JEREMY ROADRUCK
## CENTERVILLE, OHIO

As a martial arts school owner in Dayton, Ohio, I have the privilege of working with many families for over 2 decades. In addition to my experiences there I also have an extensive background through working with children and adults on a variety of issues via mentoring programs and speaking engagements, and have authored several books specializing in helping parents work with their children. As I've worked with parents and families there are a number of concerns that often come up, but the one that seems most common these days is bullying. Speaking with parents who are dealing with bullying issues has shown me firsthand how heartbreaking it can be for entire families. Knowing that your child is being hurt physically or emotionally and wanting to step in while at the same time knowing that you won't always be there to protect your children is a gut-wrenching experience for many people. I hope my participation in this project will provide some insight and strategies that may help to anyone dealing with bullying now or in the future.

**How Big a Problem is Bullying?**

Some people say that bullying isn't really as big a problem as the news and media lead us to believe, and that kids should just learn to deal with these issues as part of growing up. Then there is another group of people who see bullying as an epidemic and something that needs to be focused on and eliminated at all costs. What makes the question of how big a problem bullying is difficult to answer is that it really depends on the person in question. If the person who's being bullied is fairly confident already and the bullying isn't severe, then it might make sense to show them some "tough love" by having them face their own challenges. However, if you're dealing with someone who's insecure or scared already or who lacks the abilities to take that kind of stand, then a tough love approach won't help.

The thing is, if the child being bullied falls into the category of someone who's insecure or nervous, or who doesn't have a lot of social skills, they can internalize what's happening to them. When that happens they don't understand that the "being mean to them" part actually has very little to do with them personally. They can't see that someone being a jerk to them is actually being a jerk, they feel that they did something to deserve being treated badly, they internalize the bad feelings and see themselves as the problem. They start to take things to heart, thinking they're being treated badly because they deserve it, and it ruins their natural self-image. Even worse is that these feelings continue on through adolescence and adulthood because they never learn any different, and they feel powerless throughout their lives.

So for some people bullying may not be a big problem, and a small percentage can probably benefit from a tough love approach but they're certainly in the minority. For the larger percentage of people being bullied it is a huge problem, a lifelong problem that needs to be dealt with early on. Ignoring it or thinking it will resolve itself is a mistake parents can't afford to make.

**How Has Bullying Changed?**

One of the reasons I think some parents may have a hard time understanding how big of an issue bullying is these days is that it's not the same as when they were growing up. In past generations bullying was more face-to-face. It may have been physical or verbal, but usually the bullying happened in a certain place for a certain amount of time. The ways bullying can effect kids now is much more severe, and that has a lot to do with social media. Kids feel they can't escape the bullying, and it can follow them 24/7. Rumors can spread to an entire school at the click of a button, threats can be made from the anonymous safety of anyone's home, and bullying can happen anywhere. Between computers, cell phones, tablets, etc. bullying can be ever present in the lives of kids now.

As parents who never really had to deal with this type of bullying, the go-to answer seems to be to just ignore the social media stuff. Parents may tell kids to ignore text messages, but when you're getting texted ten to fifteen times a day or more by someone who's saying all sorts of terrible things it's really hard to ignore it. Another problem is that kids are reluctant to block the people who are doing the bullying because they live in such a connected society. Kids don't want to be bullied, but they also don't want to take the chance of being disconnected from what everyone is talking about. It's a challenge like we never had to deal with growing up, but understanding the nature of the problem can help us come up with solutions.

**Strategies to Combat Bullying**

While there is no magic bullet that can eliminate all bullying from our children's lives, I suggest a three-pronged approach to help

Bullyproof kids. The first step is to regulate and limit kids' social media diets, the second is involvement in quality activities, and the third is to read about other people's experiences. In my work I've found that these strategies, when customized for kids' specific needs, have a tremendous success rate at combating bullying.

**Strategy One: Limit Social Media**

Social media is growing, and there's no doubt that it will continue to play a major role in everyone's lives. Looking at the big picture, beyond the sheer enjoyment of it, social media can be used to network, do research, and make connections like never before. Because of the role social media plays on a global scale, it can be a great tool for people to use. Personally, I use social media myself for many reasons, but I keep everything very clean. If I see people who are critical, negative, or post things I find offensive I remove them from my news feeds. I feel that if I wouldn't have a conversation in my home because of how it makes me feel, why should I be ok with having it online?

The difference between kids and myself is that I understand the standards I have for myself, and I have the confidence to maintain those standards regardless of other people's opinions. Kids aren't born with these skills - they need to be taught. So as kids are growing up and using social media, parents should be there to teach them about what is acceptable and what isn't.

This process should start when kids are young and more accepting of parental involvement. When kids are 7 or 8 parents can introduce them to social media by letting them see the parents' social media pages. Younger kids are more likely to take this information in and learn about what is considered acceptable and what isn't. As kids get older, generally in the 5th or 6th grade, they start becoming more influenced by peers and start pushing back against parents so it's important to start teaching them before this age. 11 or 12 is about the age is when I'd start letting kids have their own social media accounts, with the understanding that parents are going to monitor it regularly for content. Once kids reach 14 or 15 I'd start to let them have some more autonomy if they can be trusted, so they have more control about what they're doing but know that I'm able to keep tabs on them. Then, at 17 or 18, they're on their own and starting their lives as adults.

Social media can be a scary thing, but it's something kids should learn about and understand so they can use it as opposed to being sucked in by it. Giving them small milestones along the way helps teach them lessons and readies them to be on their own, so they're not going into it blind or unprepared. So to recap, ages 7 through 9 kids can watch the parents on social media and talk about the different rules and standards they have and why. Then, from 10 to 12 or so, kids get their own account but the parent manages it with them. Teenagers from 14 to around 16 start earning more freedom on their accounts, and at 18 they're on their own and hopefully prepared as adults. Approaching social media in this way will help keep kids safe, and hopefully stop much of the potential bullying before it even becomes an issue.

## Strategy 2: Enroll in Quality Activities

The important term here is "quality". There are many activities kids can enroll in, but unfortunately many of them perpetuate bullying as opposed to combating it. Team sports are notorious for hazing, bullying weaker players, and generally making certain members of the team feel badly about themselves through ongoing bullying or intimidating behaviors. So when choosing an activity, parents should look for one that gives healthy lessons about conflict and how to handle it.

Personally, my recommendation for anyone looking for a quality activity is martial arts. Martial arts teaches many of the lessons parents look for in team sports like camaraderie, teamwork, dedication, perseverance, and physical fitness. It also teaches things like respect, self-esteem, confidence, and discipline. However, one of the biggest things that separates martial arts from other activities is the self-control it teaches during conflict. Martial arts teaches students how to relax, how to be calm under stress, and how to focus. This level of self-control also allows students to learn self-defense skills while simultaneously developing the confidence and control to know when and how to defend themselves and when not to. In martial arts you never speak or act out of anger because anger never controls you. This level of control and self-awareness bleeds into school, relationships, home, and anywhere else students may go. In addition to being a terrific way to maintain a healthy mental balance, it's also one of the best ways to Bullyproof a child. It gives them the confidence to stand up for themselves, the self-esteem to set high standards, and the control to not act or react out of anger.

**Strategy 3: Read About Other's Experiences**

I've found that a great way to help kids become Bullyproof is to have them read about people who have become successful in their own lives. By reading biographies or autobiographies about successful people, kids can see that even highly successful people have faced challenges in life. People who kids look up to may have had social challenges, health challenges, family challenges, or any number of others and yet they were able to find ways to get past their backstories and create great successes. These stories can help teach kids that the challenges they're facing now may be just part of their story, things to learn from so that they can come out the other side learning lessons, special knowledge, talents, and skills that will help shape their futures.

Reading these stories can start developing kids' ideas about who they want to be and how to rise above challenges. They can offer them hope and guidance and a sense that other people have gone through trials and made it through. There are so many stories parents can choose from, and they can find books that for their kids' interests. For instance, if a child is interested in science fiction, they can read about Gene Roddenberry or George Lucas. It can be a fun opportunity for the parents, too, finding stories that will interest their kids and having conversations about what they read. In this way reading these stories helps Bullyproof kids in more than one way - first, by identifying with the stories they're reading and learning lessons from them, and second by opening and maintaining the lines of communication between parents and children.

## Conclusion

Whether we're talking about bullying or any of the other issues kids may be facing in their lives, there are no easy answers for parents.  The best thing to do is try different strategies that you feel comfortable with and see what works best for you and your family.  I hope that what I've offered here helps our readers, and I'd love to offer more help to anyone who'd like it.  I'm fairly easy to find online with a simple Google search or through my website www.kungfuguyjeremy.com, and I'm always willing to engage with people who'd like to connect. I have several programs, plus I speak to youth groups, parent groups, and businesses on the topics of communication, leadership, motivation, and more.

Jeremy Roadruck is a veteran martial artist with more than 18 years of martial arts experience.

He's an accomplished competitor – nationally and internationally, winning 1st place at the Pan-American Games, and is an educator with a deep commitment and passion for developing the next generation of leaders in our communities and our country.

His deep commitment to bringing the highest quality character growth and personal development education and training to our students, instructors, staff and families is a true inspiration and powerful resource for our local community.

He is also the developer of several programs custom-tailored for specific results, such as the Falling Safely workshop – designed to teach people of all ages how to fall safely after his own mother, Barbara fell and hit her head, ending up in the ICU unconscious for 3 weeks.

Jeremy is also a published author, with his first book, ***The Kung Fu Kitties: The Adventure Begins***, which mixes the real-life rescue of a stray cat off the street with the life-lessons offered through the martial arts. His second book, ***Your Best Child Ever: Is This Game Worth Winning?*** went to #1 on Amazon.com within the first 8 hours of release.

For more information, visit www.kungfuguyjeremy.com.

# CHAPTER 2: A BULLYPROOFING FORMULA

## BY BRIAN SEETGE
## ROME, NEW YORK

Bullying is an issue that's being addressed all across the country right now which is great because it affects so many people. As owner and operator of Side Kicks Karate in Rome, New York, I've spent a lot of time focused on the mission of bullyproofing kids because it's so important to me. As someone active in the community it's been very rewarding to help spread awareness about the bullying epidemic through various public appearances and radio shows. One of my favorite things to do is visit schools myself and give bully prevention seminars where the main goal is to turn awareness into action and strive for bullyproofing everywhere.

## My Story

One of the reasons I'm so passionate about bullyproofing kids is because of my own experiences with bullying.  When I was younger I was picked on a lot for a few different things, but one of the main ones was something I had no control over.  I was born with my right leg a little shorter than my left, so when I was younger I walked with a limp and kids would pick on me and laugh.  I used to have to go to a physical therapist and one day he told my parents that I should try martial arts because the classes would work on many of the things I was doing in my sessions with him like flexibility, balance, and strength.

Enrolling me in martial arts was the best thing my parents could have done.  Physically it helped and shortly after I started lessons I didn't need physical therapy anymore, but what it gave me emotionally was even greater. Being in martial arts changed my attitude by making me more confident as a person. That confidence grew, and people at school started treating me differently. They started treating me with more respect because I had more respect for myself, and I started to feel like less of an outsider. Martial arts healed me by giving me the tools I needed to overcome the obstacles I was facing, and now I try to do the same for my students.

## How Big A Problem Is Bullying?

Even with the increased awareness about bullying there are still people who don't see it as a problem. The myth is still out there that it's not a big deal, and that if kids just ignore the problem it will go away. The truth is that bullying is a huge problem for many kids, and simply ignoring it won't help. Recent statistics show that 1 in 10 kids will be the victim of bullying, and even with more recognition of the problem it's not going away anytime soon.

Bullying is, in my opinion, a bigger problem now than it was even when I was younger. Life moves so fast now that it's affecting kids like never before, and with the increased tension and pressure to grow up there's also a lack of support and quality outside influences in kids' lives. So in addition to recognizing bullying as the major problem it is, there's also a need to recognize the need for better role models to help combat bullying.

## The Importance of Role Models

It's not something that people talk about enough, but I think children need better role models in order to aid in becoming Bullyproof. In fact, a main pillar of my bully-prevention program is in a child's support system and who they look at as role models. When I was a kid I didn't idolize a sports star or actor, my father was my role model. These days I think with all of the connectivity and social media we're missing a lot of the values that we used to have as a society and it's hurting us. Kids look at the Internet or reality TV for a guide about how to act when the people in their lives should be the examples of how they should treat others and demand to be treated. There are lots of studies on how family dynamics and a lack of strong role models can lead to a child engaging in bullying behaviors, so it's really important to consider.

What it comes down to is having a solid team behind kids, having those role models they can look up to and turn to for guidance. When I was growing up I had my parents and my martial arts instructors as my support system. If my grades dropped they'd know about it and we'd deal with it. If I got in trouble they'd get to the bottom of it and we'd talk about appropriate behavior. If I ever had any issues I was facing I knew I had a group of people who cared about me and supported me and it made it easier to come to them with problems. It's all part of the same idea of having the right support because it helped me to become the person I am today, and directed me to see how I should treat others and how they should treat me.

## Teachers Can Be Role Models, Too

I think there's a lot of mistrust toward teachers these days and it's unfortunate. Sure there are poor quality teachers out there, but I really think they're in the minority. Most teachers I've met and interacted with are dedicated to their jobs and are there to help and support kids. They're dynamic, outgoing, and consider they're profession a calling and not just a job. They truly care about their students and want to do whatever they can to ensure their success. For teachers to be great role models that's where they need to start - just show that they care and that they're available. If they do that then they become someone a kid can add to that important support system and can make a big difference in a child's life.

## Bullyproofing Formula

There are a number of things we can teach kids to help them become Bullyproof. First, teach them about bullies and how to look for them. It's ok to teach kids what bullies are and what they're looking for in a victim, and it's also ok to show them how to scan a room or an area to look for potential threats or dangers.

Next, we can teach kids to not care about what the bully is saying. I don't mean tell them to just ignore the bully and hope they go away, but to actually hear the hurtful words and really not care about them. If we teach kids that bullies can't hurt us with words because we don't believe the words they're saying then we take the power away from the bully and give it to the kid. We build up a sense of self-worth in kids so that no matter what a bully says the words don't bother them.

Another thing is we should help kids find something they're amazing at. Not good, not great, but amazing. Having something in their lives that their truly amazing at will give them something to hold onto when bullying happens. A bully can tell them they're no good, but when a child truly believes they have something that makes them special or unique they can hold onto that positive feeling in the face of adversity.

Finally, work on building that support system for your children. As parents this is a big responsibility because your kid may not come to you unless you show them how. I think in today's society even though we're more connected than ever through technology kids don't know how to really communicate emotionally. They don't know how to express themselves many times because they use social media and not face-to-face interaction. So work on communicating in real and meaningful ways and start working on developing that support system early on. Once it's in place it will be easier to maintain, but it needs constant attention.

Bullyproofing kids is something that isn't a quick or easy process, but it can be accomplished if we as parents and teachers take the time to do everything we can to help. Recognize that bullying is a problem, raise your own awareness and the awareness of other people in your children's lives, and take action to create support systems kids can rely on. If you can do those things you'll be on your way to a Bullyproof child.

Brian Seetge has been studying martial arts for over 32 years he has a 4th degree Black Belt. His goal from the age of 12 was always to run his own martial arts school and in September 1999 he opened the doors to Side Kicks Family Karate. In 1998 he was the #1 rated fighter in the PKC NY League (Professional Karate Commission) He also has numerous wins in Full Contact Kickboxing in the mid 90's

Brian and his wife Nicole have been married for three years. They have two wonderful children Kaiden Seetge (age 5) and Kameron Seetge (9 months). Kaiden is a yellow belt in his Little Ninja's Program.

His greatest skill is working with children. He has trained numerous state champions. He is one of the strongest leaders in his community. His number one goal is to empower children so they can live a happy and productive life. He has one of the best 4 to 7 year old programs for kids and specializes in working with beginners.

For more information, visit www.romenykarate.com.

# CHAPTER 3: NO SHORTCUTS TO BULLYPROOFING

## BY TODD HARRIS
## CHARLOTTE, NORTH CAROLINA

I've been training in the martial arts for over thirty years, and in that time I've accomplished a number of goals. Among these have been earning my 6th degree black belt in the World Taekwondo Federation, 7th degree black belt in Judo Kwan, and opening Martial Arts University in Charlotte, NC. While all of these accomplishments have meant a great deal to me, the thing I'm most proud of is being able stay active in the community here in Charlotte. In addition to being featured in a number of local news and radio interviews I also work with local schools and kids about bullying awareness and bullying prevention. It's a subject that's very important to me, and I hope the information I share here will help some people.

**What is Bullying?**

If we want to work on a solution to a problem we have to begin with a full understanding of what the problem is. Bullying can be confusing in many ways because it can take on so many forms, and also because some people have a different personal definition of what bullying is. For example, if a child is having a birthday party and invites all but one or two kids in the class, is that bullying? Most people would probably say no. What if it's always the same one or two kids who are purposely being excluded from the other kids' parties all year, is it bullying then?

The answers to those questions will vary depending on whom you ask, but I think that we also have to dig a little deeper. If we look at the overall effect of what being excluded has on the child being left out, the way not being included affects their confidence and self-esteem, then maybe that behavior could be considered bullying. We need to remember that bullying isn't one-dimensional – it can physical, but can be emotional, as well. Adults also tend to think of bullying in an outdated sense, where it's always one kid being physically or verbally abusive in face-to-face interactions. These days social media has made bullying something that can follow kids anywhere and can happen instantaneously, so it's a much broader issue than what parents may initially think.

## Bullying is a Problem

It's always amazing to me when I hear that people don't consider bullying to be a real problem right now. Maybe it's because many times it's less physical than adults are used to, so they don't see the evidence as easily as they would if their child came home with a bloody nose or black eye. Those types of bullying still happen, of course, but the most common bullying these days is happening on social media.  It's a problem that's running rampant, and unfortunately it often goes unnoticed by parents until it's too late.

Because of the impact of social media, I actually think that bullying is a much bigger problem now than it was in years past.  Before this technological age bullying would usually happen at school, but once a kid was home or with friends they could feel safe – there's no safety now.  Today bullying follows kids everywhere through Facebook, Snapchat, YouTube, or any of those.  It can happen in the middle of the night from someone miles away, and once a rumor or image is out there it can spread like wildfire.

**Can We Eliminate Bullying?**

The answer, quite simply, is no.  As much as I'd like to say that I think bullying is something we can eradicate completely, the truth is that negativity is part of human nature.  We've all felt negative thoughts, the difference is whether we act on those emotions or not.  Most of us have, at some point, said or done something with the intention of hurting another person.  It may not make us a bully, but it is bullying behavior that we all have the potential to demonstrate. It's ancient, and goes back to the days of Cain and Abel, so I think it would be impossible to just wipe it out altogether. However, I think that while we can't eliminate it, we can certainly put measures in place to help those who are being affected by it.

## What Can We Do?

We can't get rid of bullying, but we can do things to help alleviate its effects. The two main schools of thought on how to combat bullying are "be nice" and "be strong". The first mindset focuses on people as a whole, and tries to raise awareness about bullying in order to prevent people from acting on those negative feelings. The second mindset is more about the individual, and making that person strong enough to defend themselves mentally and physically against a bully. As a martial arts instructor I've seen the benefits of both schools of thought and think that focusing on both simultaneously gives us the best chance of helping kids become bullyproof.

We have to build kids up and make them feel confident in themselves. Not just by making them feel good, but by teaching them to respect themselves and know they're important. We have to give kids the individual self-esteem to not be affected by mean words or actions, and have the confidence to realize that their self-worth has nothing to do with what others think of them.

We also need to focus on the community around our kids and reinforce the positive behaviors we see. I've noticed that two things that people want the most and get the least of are praise and recognition. So when one child is is nice to another we should notice that behavior and comment on it, showing them that they can get attention for doing good. Too often the only way kids get noticed are when they act out, so they get the praise and recognition they desire through poor behavior. Instead I suggest that we work to change the focus and spend the time seeking out and making a bigger deal out of the times when kids are doing the right thing. So through building up confidence in individuals and praising positive behaviors in the group as a whole we can move closer to a bullyproof environment.

40

## Provide an Outlet

Whether it's in school or at home, kids need to have an outlet to talk about what's happening to them. Too often kids are being taught, especially in school, that it's wrong to run to the teacher or an adult with a problem because it makes them a tattletale. So instead of being able to seek help and guidance from people they trust, kids keep their emotions and hurt bottled inside and things just get worse. Also, if a kid does tell a teacher and nothing happens, then they're labeled a tattletale by their peers and maybe the bullying gets worse.

One of the things I like to do in my martial arts school is ask kids if somebody is doing something wrong and you tell the teacher about it, is that ok? Most of the time kids yell out, "No! That makes you a tattletale!" I tell them that where I come from that's called leadership and it should be encouraged. If somebody is doing something that's not right you shouldn't be afraid of telling someone. I explain that telling on someone just to get them in trouble is wrong, but if you're telling on someone because you know that what they're doing is wrong then that's leadership. So we have to provide an outlet for kids, let them know that telling on someone is ok, and redefine the word tattletale so that it's truly understood.

**Things That Work and Things That Don't**

There are lots of great ideas out there about how we can help make kids bullyproof. Many of them are great, but there are some that should absolutely be avoided. For me, the number one worst strategy to give to kids is telling them to just walk away if they're being bullied. Just walking away doesn't solve anything, and may actually make it worse. The bully feels more empowered because their victim hasn't retaliated in any way, and the victim feels worse because on top of being bullied they cowered away, so the emotional effects last even longer. Walking away as a strategy doesn't lead anywhere good if that's the only advice given.

So what does work? Number one, absolutely, is allowing kids to have an outlet to talk about what's happening. To do this as a parent it means maintaining good open lines of communication. Kids want to be heard, even if they don't always admit it, but these days people are so busy that taking the time to really communicate has been pushed to the side. Kids get home from school, have homework, activities, they're on their devices – sometimes it feels like there's never time to talk to your kids, to listen to what they've got to say, and to raise them the way they deserve. Trust me, with four kids of my own I know how it can be. Sometimes all I can do is tell them what to do, but other times I realize that I have to step back and take the time to listen to them and understand what's happening. If they know they can talk to me and that I'll actually listen to them it becomes much easier to have even difficult or painful conversations about what might be going on with them.

Another thing that we can do that goes along with opening up communication and listening to kids is acting on the information. If your child tells you there's an issue they need to know you'll help them get through it. That doesn't mean it will get resolved immediately, but they need to know that you'll work with them and not just brush it aside. It may mean getting teachers involved, principals, or even higher, but it's important that your kids know that they're being heard and that you're willing to do what you can to help.

**No Shortcuts**

Bullyproofing kids isn't something that will ever be easy or quick - it will always be best achieved through ongoing strategies that start young and continue through adulthood. In addition to maintaining communication, teaching kids to be empowered and recognize their self-worth is crucial to help them avoid being victimized by bullies. In my martial arts school we practice things like walking tall with confidence, good posture, and eye contact. By working on these areas consistently we're able to build and maintain high levels of self-esteem, preparing our students to face the world with a sense of confidence.

Confidence is everything, because a confidant child will be able to stand up and tell someone if another person is doing wrong. A confident child will stand up for themselves or their friends and do what is right. A confident child can look a bully in the eyes and say, "Leave me alone!" and really mean it. When you have confidence anything is possible, but we as responsible adults have to help instill that confidence in our kids. It won't be easy, it won't happen overnight, but if we take the time to work with our kids we can go a long way in making them Bullyproof.

Todd Harris began his training in the martial arts 30 years ago. Inspired by a movie that he had seen, he soon began his journey in American Karate. He graduated from East Carolina University with a degree in exercise & sport science. Todd has been featured on the cover of Martial Arts World magazine, voted #1 instructor in NC by the United States Tae Kwon Do Union, has been awarded top ten school in the US & Canada for multiple years and currently has a weekly interview on iHeartRadio.

His dedication to his students and passion to truly help others be their best is matched by none. Master Harris is married to his incredible wife Pamela Harris and they have 4 children: Danielle, Jon-Paul, Keyle and Maggie.

For more information, visit www.mauchampions.com.

# CHAPTER 4: THE BIG KID WHO GOT BULLIED

## BY VINCENT-MARCO DUCHETTA
## ARCADIA, CALIFORNIA

When you think of the kid who is being bullied at school, a lot of the time you think of a shy skinny kid. Sometimes people forget that the big kids get bullied too. As a kid growing up I was always the big kid. As an adult I'm 6'5", 280 pounds, and I grew up always being the big kid in my class. At first you may not necessarily think that the big kid would be a target for bullying, but when it comes down to it bullying is often because someone is different.

Even as an adult in my early 20's, back when I was going out to clubs, there were always the littler guys that would "mad dog" me and they'd give me "the look" like they wanted to challenge me. By that time I was already pretty well versed in martial arts and had learned how to defend myself. I'd even been on the fighting circuit with tournaments, so I didn't have any fear. Even to this day my wife finds it amusing that sometimes we'll be out on a date or something and guys will give me a hard look. She just laughs and says, "What is wrong with people? If I was a guy and saw you walking down the street, I would not give you a bad look."

Growing up, I was always a nice guy. I was nice as a kid, but as I was growing up I would get real chunky and then I would shoot up and then I would get chunkier and shoot up. Over and over again this happened to me, and I always had kids picking on me because of it. As I grew up I kind of learned with the help of God that I didn't need to put up with that, that I was strong kid and if people picked on me or hit then I needed to defend myself and fight back.

It took me a long time to do it, and 14-years-old is when I got into the worst fight I'd ever been in. The truth is, I kind of lost it and hurt a kid pretty bad. I didn't like doing it, but it was one of those things where it had to be done because I'd just taken so much for so many years. That's pretty much when the bullying stopped - when I finally stood up for myself and put an end to it.

I try to teach my own kids not to fight if it can be avoided because of course that's the last thing that we want to do. However, don't be a pushover and don't let people walk on you. Don't let people get down on you because you look different. I tell my students the same thing. Some people are skinny, some are big, some are tall, some are short, some are yellow, some are brown, and some are white. Everybody comes in different shapes, colors, and sizes but one common denominator is that we're all human; we're all people, and it's really sad when you hear about the bullying that goes on.

## Finally Standing Up for Myself

I was in the 8th or 9th grade. My dad always used to teach me how to fight, doing the old 1-2 combos on his hands. Dad wasn't a fighter, but he knew how to throw a punch. That was all I really needed at that point and it worked. When I needed to defend myself, I was able to hit the guy and that was it, it was done quickly. I paid the repercussions, though, and got suspended from school. Even though I got in trouble, the long-term effects of it were that I wasn't bullied anymore.

Reading this, I expect that, at first some people will be appalled that I'm glad that I got in a fight. Some people will think that I condone fighting, and that I teach my sons and my students that fighting is always the answer. Let me be clear, that is not what I'm saying.

Let's look at the facts, though. Statistics say that 1 in 10 kids are being bullied every single day. When we look at an average classroom of 25-30 kids, 2 or 3 kids are the targets of bullying. There has been some good news, too. For example, bullying has been on the decline since 2013 when it hit its peak. However, even if bullying incidents were to drop by half, at least 1 in 5 kids would still be being bullied.

## Bullying Is Definitely Still a Problem

When I was a kid, bullying was different. I'm 47 years old. When I grew up bullying was punching and kicking you, or pushing your bike over and name calling. It was at school, so there may have been 10-20 kids to see it, maybe 30 kids, maybe even 100 saw it if we think big. Now, today, with the presence of the online cyber bullying and all that, one kid can be destroyed in a matter of a day by tens of thousands of people chiming into this thing.

Four years ago we helped the family of a local kid who was the target of bullying. His name was Drew Ferraro. For Drew, the bullying got to be so bad for him that he jumped off of the roof of the cafeteria at school during lunch. When that little boy jumped off of the roof and ended his life you would think that the school would have been in shock - that people would have thought twice about their actions. Unfortunately you would have been wrong. You should have seen some of the comments on YouTube Facebook - people were still talking bad about him even after bullying led to his death.

**The Fine Line: Bullying vs. Kids Being Kids**

There's a fine line of when kids being kids ends and it becomes bullying, and this leads to confusion about what actually constitutes bullying. The term is used fairly loosely now in schools and with parents. 'My kid's being bullied?' 'Well, what happened to your kid?' 'Oh, somebody came up to him and twisted him and took the ball away from him.' Is that really bullying, or is that kids being kids? Does it happen every single day, day in and day out? Every day, does some kid say "Give me that ball, that's my ball," and take it away? If so, now we're talking about bullying.

A bully picks on somebody not just once but repeatedly. Using the above example, if a bully picks on little Billy every single day and takes his ball away then that is bullying. Bullying can also be repeated to different people at different times. For example, let's say the bully picks on little Billy one day, then the next day he's picking on Suzy, then the next day he's picking on Stevie. Is it one incident per kid? Yes. Are they being bullied? Yes. Because now it's happening to a bunch of kids all the time by one individual, so that makes it bullying. If it's an isolated incident, that's not bullying. That's just kids being kids and learning to live – it's not a bullying situation.

## A Simple Solution

There really is a simple solution to prevent this kind of thing from happening.  This is especially important given an atmosphere of sensitivity to liability and lawsuits.  The simple solution is proactivity, and it can be done in many ways.

A teacher can talk to the kids about bullying and be proactive about preventing it.  As teachers, coaches, parents, aunts, uncles, or just as an adult in the vicinity of a child, our job is to protect them.  Teachers can talk to their kids about the policies, be able to talk to the kids about the repercussions of bullying, and also discuss what can happen to somebody when it gets out of hand. They can share what happens to people when they're bullied and how it just doesn't make them feel good.

Of course, while teachers bear a good bit of responsibility for the safety of children in their classrooms, their effectiveness is also dependent upon alignment and agreement with the parents of their pupils. Teachers are doing their best to become knowledgeable, become educated about the signs of bullying, and put a stop to it immediately when it's seen. What about at home, though? At a Bully Prevention presentation I recently did for second and third graders, I asked this question: "Do you guys know what Facebook is?" Almost every hand went up. The next question was the shocker: "Raise your hand, how many of you have a Facebook account?" Over half the class raises their hands!

When kids are using social media such as Facebook, Instagram, and Snapchat at such a young age, it's an indication that there may be a challenge with how parents are raising their kids. Many parents are so focused on providing for their family and on their careers that this has become an era of parenting I call the "Non-Discipline Era." In over 31 years of teaching martial arts to children, I have noticed a shift in behavior of children coming into my classroom. It's happening at all ages, but I particularly notice it between the ages of 6 and 9.  There is a lack of respect and discipline and many times I see it originating in the home.

**How Martial Arts Training Helps**

Respect and discipline are two life skills that are key to children's development and growing up to be successful, whether in school or in life in general.  Both of these stem from developing self-confidence.  Martial Arts training gives somebody the confidence to stand up for themselves, and gives them the confidence to know what they can do protect themselves. It doesn't matter what system of martial arts you teach or what you study or learn - I think martial arts are all great in their own way. No matter what style you learn, it gives you the confidence to be able to walk away or to stand up to a bully, and ultimately to defend yourself appropriately.  Obviously, part of the training is the ability to defend yourself physically and actually put your hands on somebody. Of course we teach students that fighting is that last resort, but being able to have the knowledge and confidence to stand up for yourself and stand up for others is very important. I think that the martial arts gives students that aspect, it gives them the confidence, the ability to able to walk away.

One of our rules and our studio rules that we have hanging on our reads: "Do not use any of the techniques learned at this school, except to protect the well-being of yourself or the defenseless."

When this idea and philosophy is instilled into our students they change the way they act. When you understand this rule, you become confident in the fact that you don't need to pick on anybody because you've learned how to defend yourself. Further, the transformation is not only in the way they carry themselves because confidence carries into all areas of life. Kids who train in martial arts start doing well on their school work, they start doing well in their everyday life, and they learn that you don't need to pick on anybody because you have the confidence.

In the end, a bully is just a coward.  A bully is a guy who doesn't

really know who to make friends and many times his behavior is

an attempt to become friends with people. Yes, he's attracting the

wrong friends, but that's how he gets attention.


**Giving Your Child the Right Tools**


If your child is being bullied, or is a potential target of bullying, the

solution is very easy - help your children become confident in

themselves.  Of course I am biased to martial arts programs, but

it's all about giving a child the feeling that he or she isn't alone, and

that they can stand up for themselves.


When your child is able to have that and feel that, then they can

truly be bullyproof.

Vincent-Marco Duchetta owns and operates Elite Youth Sports After School Program and Summer Camps at Ring of Fire Martial Arts Academy located in Arcadia, CA. Mr. Duchetta has been helping kids in the San Gabriel Valley area of Southern California for over 20 years by teaching them the art of Hapkido. Mr. Duchetta has been an award winning speaker at many of the area schools and his Academy has won numerous people's choice awards locally for their ongoing support in the anti bullying and self defense programs they sponsor as well as teach at.

For more information, visit www.rofmaa.com.

# CHAPTER 5: WORKING THE CONFIDENCE

## BY JAKE MIESNER
## SHREVEPORT, LOUISIANA

Moving can be tough for a child, and moving during the middle of the school year makes it even worse. Not only is a kid trying to figure out his place, where he's at, and who is who, but it's all at a time when seemingly everyone else fits in their place.

This is how bullying started for me. I was raised in a nice town in Oklahoma that was pretty inclusive of all people. In the middle of the fourth grade I moved to a town in Texas that was more "cliquish", or exclusive of certain people.

There was good news, however. Before classes started up for the spring semester I found that there was another boy that lived on my block who was about my age. He was a nice kid, and he was nice to me, so I befriended him.

When classes started I realized that other kids didn't consider him to be "cool". In fact, he was actually the one that was being bullied at school by "the cool kids". Since he was nice to me I tried to do my best to stick up for him. That's what put me in their sights - the bullies wouldn't have noticed me if I hadn't tried to step in and stick up for him.

That set in motion a period of about 3 or 4 years of me going back and forth with these bullies each day. I wasn't a very physical kid and I'd never been in a fight, but when dealing with the bullies I tried everything I was taught in school. I tried to shut them down with my words, I tried to stand up to them, and I let them know I wasn't going to back down. They just kept pushing and pushing until the point came that they wanted to see what I would physically do. They wanted to fight, and whenever that point came I usually ran. You know, bullies don't usually pick on people in a 1-on-1 environment so I ran, and ran fast!

## Making Friends with the Bullies?

A few years into it we were in the 7th grade, which was the time where you could start doing athletics and be part of the school's sports programs. A lot of the guys were going out for the football team, and it was basically the guys who were already the tough kids, the cool kids, including the bullies.

So I thought, "If there's any chance for me to shut this down, it's to get on the same team so they'll see we're all on the same side." So I went out for the football team and made it, but instead of helping to stop the bullying all it did was change the location to the locker room. Since the bullies were all on the team together they were constantly around me, and being slammed up against metal lockers did NOT seem safer than outrunning them in an open environment.

## Learning to Take Care of Myself

When I realized that I wasn't safe anymore I asked my parents to enroll me in martial arts. At that age, I understood myself enough to know that I wanted to learn how to fight back and stand up for myself. So my parents found a great martial arts school and a terrific instructor whom I loved.

My parents told the instructor that I was being bullied and wanted to learn self-defense so I could fight back when they tried to come after me. When I started taking lessons my instructor told me, "I'll teach you how to protect yourself, but I don't want you ever using this stuff. If you use what I teach you, and I find out you've been getting in fights at school, you're out of the program. I won't teach you anymore." Well, shoot! This guy was going to teach me how to protect myself, but I wasn't allowed to use it.

I wanted to stay with him and keep learning just in case I ever had to use what I was learning, but he really pressed the point to try every other option *before* any kicking or punching. So what ended up happening was I got a lot faster at outrunning the bullies and riding my bicycle faster than a group of five or six kids chasing me, because I did everything I possibly could to avoid using martial arts. That was my education through bullying.

## The Jock Who Changed It All for Me

In my 9th grade year I was 14 and tested for my black belt in Taekwondo. I had a really vigorous black belt exam where I had to test with the adults. In preparing for my test, what I didn't realize was how tough my instructor had really made me. It was an impressive display of skills and someone, (not me), spread the word around the school when I passed the test.

In high school, the bullying had slowed down because we were in different social circles and had different things to worry about.

The jocks hung with other jocks and I hung around with musicians and band kids.

A new jock moved in during our freshman year and bumped into me in the hall between classes. He pushed me up against the lockers and was about to start a fight with me. One of his buddies, one of my past bullies, stopped him and said, "Dude, he's got a black belt. You don't want to mess with him." I was thinking, "Cool! I don't even have to use martial arts because word's gotten out." That event was when everything changed for me.

To this day I have never had to use a kick or a punch to defend myself. Even though that's why I started learning martial arts, my instructor's philosophy kept me avoiding every scenario that might lead to a situation with the bullies. I did get a lot faster running and biking away from trouble, but never learned to deal with it.

## What I Learned From All of This

Seven or eight years after high school, I returned to my hometown and ran into a girl that I knew from my school days. She was married to one of the guys who was essentially the head bully in my younger life. Once she told me that, I said, "Oh my goodness! I can't believe you married him. He wasn't nice to anyone back in school." She said that they'd been discussing his youth lately, and he had admitted to bullying me and other kids. She said he mentioned my name and a few others that he felt really bad about. Upon reflecting about WHY he bullied others, the discussion came back to his rough home life. Apparently, his dad used to beat him and since he couldn't stand up to his dad or stop him he acted out toward others at school. I don't think he told anyone about his home life while going through it. She said that he felt terrible about bullying us and wished he could apologize to us.

That gave me a deeper understanding of why everything happened, and it also made me pity him. It made me wish we could've been friendly enough with each other that maybe he would have opened up to me and I could have helped him. I'm not saying that I could have or would have stood up to his father myself, but I would like to think I could have guided him away from that trouble. Regardless, the conversation opened my eyes. It helped me look at bullying from another perspective and gain more understanding.

**Bullying Is a Growing Problem**

Despite opinions from some people who think bullying isn't a big issue, the statistics argue otherwise. Today, studies report that 75% of kids under 18 are affected by bullying. This is even higher than when I was going through school, so the statistics prove that bullying is a growing problem.

With technology like we have today there are many more outlets for people to pick on kids or isolate their peers, via channels such as social media or texting. Bullying is part of human society - something that's always been around and that I believe will always be around. I don't think we'll ever abolish all bad family situations that may lead to bullying behavior. On top of that, with the increase in technology it doesn't look as though the opportunities to hurt others will be decreasing.

The good news is that there are numerous anti-bullying programs in existence today, as well as growing awareness of the issue in schools. I believe that schools will be key areas to show bully prevention effectiveness in the future.

I've been a teacher in public schools, working with kids on junior high and high school campuses. A few years ago I witnessed a fight break out between two boys in the hall outside my classroom. Another teacher and I had to separate the boys and break up the fight. Even while stopping the fight, I was more worried about losing my job by putting my hands on a student than I was about stopping the fight. The other teacher actually got hit by one of the boys while separating them, and we agreed afterward that we would probably get in more trouble than the boys fighting. That's where society has gotten us to, lately. Teachers have become more limited in their abilities to discipline and protect students. Even so, not all hope is lost.

## The Most Powerful Weapon for Teachers

There is still hope for teachers to prevent bullying in the classroom. The most powerful weapon that teachers have in their arsenal comes from the nature of the relationships they have with their pupils.

Sometimes students spend more time with their teachers than they do with their own parents. Kids stay eight hours a day - sometimes more due to extracurricular activities at schools. As a band director I definitely spent a lot of time with my kids, and some kids spent more time at the band hall than they did at home. All that time around students helps a teacher learn more about their students and what's going on in their lives. It's easy to develop a "baseline" for each student's personality and notice when they start acting different than the norm. This knowledge of our students' personalities is the most powerful weapon teachers have in our arsenal. This will help us notice when they're not acting normal so we can raise the issue & address any concerns before they become a problem.

Some students even hung around my band hall that weren't in band. They'd come hang out when they didn't have a ride home or didn't want to go straight home. They knew it was open and safe, so I was even able to get to know students that weren't in my classes. Whether it was the relaxed atmosphere of the band hall or my demeanor, some of those other kids would open up to me about what was going on in their lives. This is a common occurrence for teachers. With statistics stating that 75% of kids under 18 are affected by bullying, it's safe to say that educators have access to kids who are either being bullied themselves, are friends with a bullying victim, or have seen bullying in action. If teachers observe their students and keep an open line of communication with the parents then hopefully we can all help catch and address these issues before they become too big to overcome.

## Working the Confidence

It's pretty common knowledge that bullies will try to pick on someone who looks weaker – someone who doesn't look like they're walking or moving with confidence. Someone who looks weak or like an "easy target" is much more likely to be bullied. In an effort to help yourself or your kids, one simple tactic is to start working on confidence by trying to look more confident, act more confident, and eventually *be* more confident. There's a saying that goes, "Fake it 'til you make it." This means at least *act* it even if you don't truly *feel* it.

Another solution, especially good for your kids, would be to find programs and people that will help develop confidence. I'm not suggesting enrolling them in a sport that's going to give trophies to everybody who participates, because to develop real confidence they need to see that they can succeed and that they're worth something. For me, that came through learning self-defense and participating in martial arts. Martial arts are an individual sport, so all trophies won at tournaments and all successes at belt testing were won on my own merit. Growing up I participated in all sorts of sports, and that was fine. I knew I could kick a soccer ball, throw a baseball, and dribble a basketball, but all games were lost or won as a team. Trophies were given to both the star athletes and the weaker players sitting the bench, which didn't help build my confidence at all. Martial arts, as an individual sport, helped me prove what I could do on my own.

Having served our youth as both a school teacher and a martial arts instructor, it is clear that this problem of bullying continues on generation to generation. It may look different from parent to child, but the solutions are the same as they've always been. People need to be more confident, and parents and teachers need to be more engaged with their kids. By doing this, although we may never eliminate bullying, we can help protect and guide our kids.

Jake Miesner has been involved in martial arts for 25 years, and has been teaching for more than 20 years. His martial arts background includes training in Taekwondo, Japanese Jiu-Jitsu, & others. As a martial artist, Jake has consistently performed & competed at high levels around the US.

Professionally, Jake has a degree in Education, which he has used to teach in public schools at the Middle School & High School levels. He has also taught at the College/University level (after achieving his Master's Degree). Jake enjoys teaching & passing on knowledge of "how to teach" to his students, building the next generation of educators.

# CHAPTER 6:
# WHAT WORKS AND DOESN'T

## BY JESSE BERNAL
## AURORA, COLORADO

In my experience of over 25 years practicing martial arts I've had the pleasure of working with many families. A common concern heard from a great number of them is about bullying. At Colorado Martial Arts Academy I teach my students Tang Soo Do. More importantly, I teach bullyproofing strategies to the students and families who come through my doors. Bullying is a difficult challenge for anyone to face, but there are ways that people can work to overcome this issue if it comes into their lives.

## Bullying Then and Now

Bullying isn't a new. Many adults witnessed, or experienced it growing up. I'm sure, many even dealt with their own bullies. I know, I did. That being said, the way bullying happens has changed over the years. When I was young bullying was seen as something of a rite of passage, and parents weren't nearly as involved as they seem to be now. Many times the only advice a parent would give to a child being bullied was that they had to stand up for themselves, which made sense, because the majority of bullying was physical. One kid would push another one around in the schoolyard and the one being pushed around may eventually stand up for him or herself, but regardless the bullying behavior would usually end when the school day ended. It was physical and required face to face contact.

Nowadays there's no escape, thanks to cyberspace. Social media has made it so bullying isn't just physical, but can also be deeply emotional and devastating to a child on many levels. In addition, society seems to have moved into a mindset where the schools and parents have an intense aversion to any kind of physicality at all. This, to me, has actually taken away some of the tools kids need to defend themselves. Because physical altercations are so taboo now, emotional bullying is even more prevalent. In the past kids may have been able to address things in a physical way to stop them before they got too intense, kids are now being held to a zero tolerance policy on physical contact while the other types of bullying, emotional and social, are running rampant. We see this happening more often as schools attempt to avoid lawsuits by suspending or expelling kids at the first sign of physicality, which often further isolates a bulling victim, reinforcing their feeling that they don't have a way out of their situation. In fact, many times schools seem to turn a blind eye to bullying in order to save themselves the headaches that may come from dealing with the issue head on.

I had a personal experience with how schools respond to bullying with my own children. Soon after we moved to Colorado my children began being bullied. There was physical bullying that included sexual harassment as well as social and emotional bullying.  As a parent I felt extremely disappointed in the school's response to the bullying and felt like we had no support from the administration.  My Wife and I made the decision to take our kids out of that school and enroll them in a different one, telling the school exactly why we made that decision.  I also made it a point to explain to my children what bullying is, how to avoid bullying, and why some kids become bullies.

## Why Do Kids Bully?

I wish there was an easy answer to why some kids bully, but it's pretty complicated and there are many theories.  One of the most common is that it has to do with power.  The child doing the bullying wants to feel powerful and they do that by victimizing someone they perceive as being weaker than themselves.  This ties into another theory that many bullies come from abusive homes, and the power they exert over others is a direct response to the lack of power or control they feel in their own lives.  In some cases the bully has convinced themselves that the victim somehow deserves to be bullied or abused.

While all of these theories hold water, one that I'm particularly drawn to is based on simple impulse control. Kids tend to have poor impulse control and gravitate toward things they think will be fun or feel good at the time with little to no consideration of consequences for themselves or others. When kids bully, many times it's because they get a rush from the act. Put simply, it makes them feel good. There's no complicated thought process where a bully thinks, "I'm unhappy, so let me make someone else unhappy, and then I'll feel better." That's more complex than what actually happens. A bully doesn't think, "If I make someone else feel bad about themselves I'll feel better", they just think, "If I do this thing, I feel better". They don't have an incredibly deep level of introspection or reasoning for their behavior, they're just engaging in actions that make them feel better. When a person has hunger pains, they eat. Bullying behavior is sustenance for the emotional pain of the bully. Temporary relief for their "hunger". It's an intentional and ongoing pattern of behavior, and that's what makes them a bully.

## How Schools Handle Bullying

While it's true that social media has created another layer to bullying, kids still deal with bullying at school. It's a place where they spend a huge portion of their lives surrounded by peers, so it would be foolish to think bullying doesn't happen there. When I think of how schools deal with the bullying they do see the first word that comes to mind is inadequate. Part of it has to do with the litigious nature of our society. You might assume that because of potential lawsuits schools would be more likely to end bullying as soon as possible, but what happens many times is that fear of legal action actually creates an atmosphere of disengagement. Teachers and administrators remain as hands off as they can in order to avoid being pulled into lawsuits.

Because their hands are in many ways tied, teachers who want to take a stand against bullying should do what they can when they can. One thing they can do is be willing to listen to kids who come forward about bullying and try to be as fair and impartial as possible. Teachers need to get as much information as they can and document anything they find. Bullying can't be condoned and shouldn't be ignored. Even if administration has tied a teacher's hands that teacher can still gather information and present what they have as a way to help. Doing something is better than doing nothing.

## Steps Parents Can Take

Obviously, schools aren't perfect. Kids do spend a lot of time under the care of teachers, it's the parents who have to be most diligent in the bullyproofing process. The first thing parents need to do is understand what bullying is. Once they understand the definition of bullying it makes identifying and dealing with it much easier. The correct way to define bullying is that it's when a person purposely tries to harm another person physically, socially, or emotionally. It has to be purposeful, and if a person truly doesn't realize what they're doing then it's not technically classified as bullying. Next, the behavior has to be repetitive. Even if it's just twice it may be considered bullying depending on the severity. So intent and repetition are the key pieces to defining bullying. Once parents have that information they can work on strategies.

The number one strategy parents can use to help combat bullying, is to make sure kids know they can come to them with any issues they're having. Kids need to know that if they come to you, you're going to listen. Even if you're not able to take action immediately to resolve the issues, you will always pay attention. Your kids need to know that they have a safe place to talk and let things out. Recently, I was speaking with a retired school psychologist and he told me that the main reason many kids don't report bullying sooner is because they feel ashamed. They think their parents will be disappointed in them for letting themselves be bullied, so the onus really is on the parents to start open and honest dialogue early on, making sure kids know they can always come forward with any problems. That doesn't mean just checking in once in a while, it means constantly reassuring kids that home is a safe place and they can always talk about anything that's happening with them. Starting and maintaining that level of communication will go a long way in bullyproofing our kids.

Another thing parents can do is work on building up kids' self-confidence. Bullies pick on people they think deserve it and who look like easy targets. If a child exudes self-confidence they become difficult to isolate and they won't look like good targets for bullies. Self-confidence also helps kids form strong friendships so they're surrounded by a sort of community of support. Bullies are more likely to go after loners because they don't want to deal with an entire group. There are lots of ways to help kids find a sense of community and forge strong friendships. Sports teams and other activities are great, but I highly recommend martial arts. Quality martial arts academies are terrific places for kids to develop their self-confidence and be part of a group that will support and encourage positive behaviors and attitudes.

## What Not to Do

With so many so-called "experts" out there, there are bound to be some bad ideas circulating for how to deal with bullying. One of the worst and most common I hear is the "just ignore it" strategy. This doesn't work because a bully will take a victim's passive attitude as permission to continue the behavior. As the bully learns that there aren't any repercussions for their behavior, they'll continue and even escalate it because no one is stopping them. This ties into understanding the definition of bullying and maintaining open communication with kids. If those strategies are being followed a parent should never even speak the words "just ignore it".

Another ineffective strategy is telling a child to make friends with a bully. Telling a victim to become friends with a person who's tormenting them is ridiculous and extremely difficult. The bully will see this offer of friendship as another sign of weakness and an invitation to continue the behavior. Also, why would you want your child trying to be friends with someone who thinks it's ok to treat them horribly? I know the idea of making friends is probably coming from a good place, but it's really a terrible idea.

Finally, another well intended, but trap filled strategy parents may use is having a child report bullying behavior to a teacher or administration without parental involvement. Parents need to be advocates for their children, especially when it comes to their children having to deal with other adults. In this case dealing with other adults may also mean marks on a permanent record, emotional, physical or social retaliation from the accused, and possible future issues with safety. Children shouldn't be expected to deal with teachers, administration, or the red tape of bullying alone - a parent telling them to see a principal or a teacher without becoming involved themselves is a recipe for disaster.

## Keep At It

Bullying isn't something that's going to ever completely go away. That doesn't mean we should allow our kids to be victims or face challenges completely alone. Start conversations about bullying with your kids early on and keep those conversations going throughout their lives. Do whatever you can to help build up the self-confidence in your kids and get them involved in activities that reinforce the idea of community and friendship. Above all, be involved in the important areas of your children's lives and never assume they can be Bullyproof on their own...they need your help,

even if they don't act like it.

With 25 years of experience, Jesse Bernal's love for martial arts started as a child watching Kung Fu and Samurai movies. It wasn't until he was an adult that he began training in Tang Soo Do.

When he's not teaching or practicing Tang Soo Do, Mr. Bernal is kept busy with his wife, Shawnna and his 13 year old twins.

"I'm honored each time an adult decides they want me to help them or their children discover what makes Martial Arts so great."

"I believe Martial Artists have a greater responsibility to the community than your average citizen. Training in a Traditional Martial Art like Tang Soo Do, we place an emphasis on the development of Mind, Body & Spirit; not just for self improvement, but to help the people around us."

For more information, visit www.aurorakarate.com.

# CHAPTER 7:
# NO EASY WAY OUT

## BY JOSE MONTERO
## OCALA, FLORIDA

When I started training in the martial arts over thirty-five years ago I had no idea how important it would end up being for me. Through my years of training I've had many amazing opportunities as a result of my involvement in the martial arts, including competing both nationally and internationally. For nearly twenty years my focus has shifted to spending my time helping children and families experience martial arts and today I run Ocala ITF Taekwondo Academy in Ocala, Florida. At my academy we spend a lot of time working on helping kids become bullyproof and it's an issue I'm very passionate about.

## The Big Deal About Bullying

Even with the tremendous amount of media coverage about bullying there are still people out there who don't believe it's a big deal. Unfortunately, when it comes to those people I don't think anything will sway their opinions. As it is there are steady reports coming out about kids being bullied to the point of hurting themselves or committing suicide, so for someone to say bullying doesn't exist or it isn't a big issue seems absurd to me.

In my opinion bullying is one of the worst things in the world for someone to go through. It can hurt on a physical or emotional level, and its effects can last for years for a victim. As a martial arts instructor I've seen the effects first hand with students who have been bullied to the point of not even wanting to get out of bed in the morning because of what's happening to them. It's a problem that impacts children, adults, and even whole families. If we don't raise awareness then the problem will continue to get worse, but I'm optimistic that with the right strategies and awareness we can actually eliminate bullying someday.

## How Bullying Has Changed

Bullying has changed a lot over the years and I think that may be part of the reason some people don't understand how dangerous it can be now. I was bullied myself as a child, but when I was a kid bullying was mainly physical and fairly isolated. Typically someone would get pushed around or picked on at school, and the bullying would end once the school day ended.

This still happens, but it goes far beyond that now. Bullying no longer stays within a few feet of the bully, it can travel anywhere almost instantaneously. With social media like Snapchat, Facebook, or Twitter, kids are more connected than ever before which means bullying can reach further than ever before. Instead of having to pick on someone face to face a bully can do it from anywhere. Instead of home being a safe place to escape from bullies, kids now face the challenge of bullying being able to follow them anywhere and spread to the entire world in mere seconds.

## Strategies for Bullyproofing

To me the number one strategy we can give our kids to help them become bullyproof is to build up their confidence. There are many ways to do this but one that I highly recommend is increasing their physical activity. I mentioned that social media is a big factor in bullying and that's because kids seem to be attached to their devices all the time. When I was a kid we were more active and were outside playing instead of sitting on Facebook or playing video games. One way to reduce the influence of social media is to encourage kids to break away from it more, and by encouraging physical activity you get the added bonus of improving physical fitness and confidence, which are great ways to move toward a bullyproof life.

I realize that my opinion may be a bit biased, but I think martial arts is one of the best ways for kids to get some physical activity and build their confidence at the same time. Martial arts teach many things beyond simple punching and kicking. There is of course that side of it, and it's important for children to learn how to defend themselves and have the confidence to do so if necessary. However, martial arts also teach confidence through mental training along with the physical training. Students learn how to focus, how to assess a dangerous situation and react without panicking, and what appropriate reactions are. They have the confidence to stand up for themselves and defend themselves in the way that each individual situation calls for, and this confidence clearly defines them as people who will not be easy targets. That piece is important because bullies don't want to pick on someone who's going to fight back or stand up to them, they want someone who will panic or get scared and remain an easy target.

Just as I have a favorite strategy for bullyproofing kids I also have a least favorite. I know that different ideas work for different people, but one strategy I see as being extremely ineffective is telling kids to just walk away from a bully. Walking away is problematic because it doesn't resolve anything. If a child is being bullied and walks away, the situation will get worse because in the bullies mind their victim now looks weaker. Walking away may not even work because a bully can follow or corner a child, and the child is now left with no other options because they haven't been taught any. Even if walking away does work it will only be short-term because the child will have to cross that bully's path again soon, and the bullying will continue.

## The Role of Teachers

Even though bullying has evolved in many ways it still has a very strong presence in schools. Kids spend as many as six or eight hours a day in school, even longer in some cases, so of course bullying will occur. Since we can't be with our kids throughout the entire day we have to put a lot of trust in teachers to help protect our kids from bullying, and unfortunately because of different rules and restrictions teachers may actually have very limited power. Sadly this means that quite often teachers end up ignoring troublesome behavior because they feel as though their hands are tied.

While it's true that teachers may not have as much power as they, or parents, would like sometimes, they can still do a lot to help kids become bullyproof. A first step is refusing to ignore any behavior they find troubling. They should do what they can to nip behavior in the bud, even if it means documenting and getting parents or administrators involved.

Teachers should also let kids know in no uncertain terms that they're available to help if needed. Kids who lack confidence may not even have enough in them to tell a teacher if they're being hurt, so teachers should be going out of their way to make sure kids know they can come to them with any issues they're facing. Just knowing their voices will be heard may be enough to encourage a child to come forward who's experiencing bullying.

Finally, teachers should try to continually become more educated about bullying. Reading about bullying, attending seminars, inviting guest speakers into the class, or creating anti-bullying initiatives are all ways teachers can help their students to be bullyproof. There's an amazing amount of information out there to go through, and being aware of new research and studies may help teachers to make better decisions about how they'll choose to handle bullying in their own classroom.

**No Easy Way Out**

There are times when parents come to me and are very frustrated by their child being bullied. They may ask what can they do to stop the behavior right away, or if there's one single thing they can do that will help eliminate bullying from their child's life. I wish there was a simple way to help a child end bullying right away but the reality is there is no easy way out. It's an ongoing process that must continue throughout someone's life in order to make them truly bullyproof.

There is also no single strategy or technique that will work every time for every person being bullied. Tools that work for one person may not work for another, and something that does work once may not work in a different situation. Because of this it's important for us to give our kids as many strategies as we can so they have a number of tools in their toolbox to choose from, and also to teach them how to use those tools effectively for when they're needed. That's another reason I believe martial arts are a great way to bullyproof kids, because we work on developing so many different mental and physical strategies for kids to use if they're bullied. At the end of the day it's really all about the support kids get from the adults in their lives, though, so we need to keep working together to do everything we can to help our kids become and stay bullyproof for life.

Javier Montero is the owner and instructor at Ocala ITF Taekwondo in Ocala, Florida.

Having trained in Taekwondo for decades, Javier dedicates his life today to sharing martial arts with children and adults, to spread the life skills that great martial arts teaches.

An international champion, Javier continues to train and compete, while encouraging his own students to better themselves in life, particularly in the area of bullying.

"If we look back in time, many kids lived in agony because they were bullied causing some of them to commit suicide. We as Martial Arts instructors, have this responsibility of helping the weak to become strong not only physically but mentally as well. Also we need to educate the bullies for them to realize how bad this is in society."

For more information visit www.ocalaitftaekwondo.com.

# CHAPTER 8: BULLYING CAN BE BENEFICIAL

## BY DANIEL GRYCZKA
## PARKLAND, FLORIDA

Being involved in martial arts for nearly twenty-five years and

being the owner of Karate Zone in Parkland, Florida has given me

the opportunity to see up close and personal the effects bullying

can have on people. As someone who was bullied myself this

subject is something I'm very passionate about, and I've dedicated

my life to doing what I can to help as many people as possible become more aware of bullying and capable of defending themselves.

Bullying, to me, is a huge problem right now and it's becoming more prevalent all the time. In order to really get into a conversation about how to bullyproof kids we have to start with an understanding of what bullying is. My definition of bullying has three components. First, it has to be intentional. People can accidentally hurt someone else's feelings, but to be a bully they have to willfully be engaging in the behavior and fully aware of what they're doing. Second, the behavior has to be recurring. If someone acts mean one day or once in a while then that's a person having a bad day. We all have bad days - that doesn't make us a bully. Finally, there has to be some sort of harm involved for it to be considered bullying. If someone gives you a dirty look over and over and they do it on purpose does that make them a bully? Probably not, because other than receiving a dirty look you're not being harmed. However, the harm in bullying doesn't have to be just physical harm - it could be mental or social as well. So to recap, for something to be labeled bullying it has to be intentionally done more than once for the purpose of causing another person harm.

## My Experience with Bullying

I mentioned that I've been bullied myself in the past. I actually think most people have experienced bullying at some point in their lives, as kids or even adults, and for me it happened when I was young and was the new kid in school. In addition to being new I was also really tall so I stood out, and for kids anything that stands out is going to attract attention. On top of that I was shy. So I was a tall, skinny, shy new kid and when I started getting picked on I had no idea how to deal with it. I also got picked on for having big ears and a big forehead - really anything physical. Since I wasn't prepared to deal with it I just took it even though it made me feel terrible, and since the bullies could see how their words hurt me they kept coming after me. I also felt horrible because the things they were teasing me about were things I had no control over, so I took it all very personally since I had no concept of how to deal with the situation.

Fortunately for me I was eventually introduced to martial arts and that's what helped me to break the cycle I was stuck in. I was accepted in an environment where encouragement and self-esteem were a focus, and my confidence finally started to get built up to where it needed to be to be able to overcome my bullying. In addition to the emotional confidence I was also given physical confidence as I learned how to defend myself if that's what was needed. Just knowing that I had the ability to defend myself gave me a tremendous boost of confidence and really helped me leave the paralyzing fear I was experiencing in the past. This experience showed me that mental confidence is a great tool to use in bullyproofing, especially when combined with physical self-defense instruction.

## Bullying Changes

My experience with bullying was just that - my experience. Bullying is different for everyone, and time has actually changed the face of bullying quite a lot. When I was younger bullying was very much a face-to-face ordeal whether it was physical or verbal.

Nowadays with social media bullying can happen anywhere and at any time, making it even more devastating for kids to deal with. I think that some adults and parents still look at bullying the way they did when they were younger and underestimate the impact it can have when a child being bullied literally can't escape it no matter how far away they go. For these reasons it's more important than ever to continue to focus on awareness and teach our kids strategies that will help them to be more safe.

**Strategies for Bullyproofing: Teachers**

When discussing how to bullyproof kids it's important to take time to think about the impact schools and teachers have. Kids are in school six or more hours every day for most of the year and while they're there the teachers are the adults who we trust to protect them. My wife is actually a schoolteacher and we have conversations often about what she thinks of bullying and her perspective on things. She's shared with me time and time again that the notion that many teachers have limited power to deal with bullying because of their administration's policies is true.

Teachers who have the backing and support of their administrators can be a lot more productive when bullying issues arise, but when that doesn't happen the best way teachers can help kids become bullyproof is to just be good, caring teachers and try to maintain a classroom that is controlled. Some teachers literally only have control over what happens within the walls of their class, so doing everything they can to prevent bullying behaviors from even starting and keeping a disciplined classroom may be their best option.

Another thing teachers can do, if they have the resources, is to seek help from outside sources. Tapping into a school's behavioral therapists for insight is great because oftentimes they'll have ideas or strategies that may have new research supporting their effectiveness. Teachers can also seek outside speakers to visit their classroom and aid in the bullyproofing through talks and presentations. I know many martial arts school owners, for example, who visit classrooms on an ongoing monthly basis in order to share bullyproofing ideas and lessons with the class. Teachers have a very difficult job to do and an incredible amount on their plates, so any outside help for extra things like bully prevention could be very powerful.

## Strategies for Bullyproofing: Parents

I said earlier that bullying is a little different for everyone. No one's experience will be exactly the same, and so a variety of strategies are necessary to work on in order to prepare kids as much as possible to deal with bullies. Some tactics are age specific, some won't be natural or comfortable for kids no matter how many times they practice, so we need to give them as many tools in their toolboxes to choose from so when the time comes they can use the one that works best for them. That being said there are some strategies that I find effective for most kids to learn.

First, I think that the "walk away" strategy can be effective, but only if done properly. If a child is bullied and from the first time it happens they choose to ignore the behavior and simply not care about it, the bully may just stop. This isn't to say that a child should walk away with their head down or feeling bad - it only works if they can recognize that the words of a bully mean nothing to them and have no effect on their lives. Having the confidence and self-respect to be able to pull of this strategy doesn't come naturally for many kids, though, so it's crucial that parents practice and reinforce the confident actions and mindset. If done right this can nip a bully's actions in the bud because the "victim" refuses to feed into the behavior and the bully doesn't get any satisfaction.

While walking away is a very peaceful way to react to bullying, sometimes it's not enough. If a bully actually puts their hands on another kid and tries to hurt them then I am all for instructing a child to defend themselves. Too often we try to tell kids to ignore behavior that's causing them harm because we don't want to encourage fighting, but in the process we're telling kids it's ok for other people to hurt them and for them to just take it. I don't think that's ok and it's not how I want my students to grow up. Of course we want our kids to be kind and respectful, but not at the risk of being hurt physically or emotionally in ways that may stay with them for years after.

## Bullying Can Be Beneficial

I know that heading may rile some readers up as soon as they read it, but allow me to explain. Some people talk about how bullying can be eliminated or how great a world without bullying would be but I have a slightly different take on it. First of all I don't think that bullying will ever be eliminated from our lives. It's been around for a very long time and will be around for longer still because it's a part of who we are as humans. I also think that eliminating bullying altogether could cause a different type of problem where kids don't learn how to stand up for themselves socially, physically, emotionally, or any other way. Sometimes I think that we want such good and happy lives for our kids that we end up taking away opportunities for them to grow and learn about falling down and picking themselves up on their own. Having to deal with bullies and going through that process can tell someone a lot about themselves and actually end up being a positive thing for their character.

## No Quick Fixes

Recognizing the potential benefit of bullying in no way means that I would encourage bullies or bullying behavior, but I'm choosing to acknowledge the reality as opposed to ignoring it. Bullies are going to happen and as parents and adults it's up to us to decide how we're going to prepare our kids to face the challenges we know are out there. Instead of trying to eliminate bullying I'd advocate for teaching kids how to redirect or deal with their problems directly. Instead of trying to give short-term band-aids for bullying I'd prefer to teach tactics that will be practical in the real world and serve as life lessons even into adulthood. Bullying is a real and complex issue, but if we all work together to stay aware and assertive then we can help make bullyproof kids that will also become bullyproof adults.

Daniel Gryczka has spent years teaching families and children martial arts in the Parkland, Florida area. His martial arts school, Karate Zone, focuses on life skills such as Focus, Confidence, Discipline, and Independent Motivation. His students use these character traits at home, school and everywhere they go.

For more information, visit www.thekaratezone.com

# YOUR NEXT STEP: DECISION AND ACTION

One of my favorite quotations from Anthony Robbins is the following:

*"It is in our moments of decision that our destiny is shaped."*

And what a powerful quotation that is. The roots of the word "decision" mean "to cut off." This says that when you or I make a decision about something, we cut off all other options.

After reading this volume, what decision are *you* going to make about bullying?

Are you going to seek to empower more kids?

Are you going to enroll your child in a sport or activity that helps them feel like a superhero?

Are you going to your local elementary school and going to volunteer?

Or something else?

Not only is making the *decision* important, but taking the *follow-up actions* is really what will make the difference in your life, and the lives of kids in our community dealing with bullying.

Our decisions shape our destiny. Our actions sculpt our lives.

Go out there and make magic happen for you and our world.

118

# GETTING INVOLVED WITH THE BULLYPROOF PROJECT

The *Bullyproof: Unleash the Hero Inside Your Kid* book series is designed to raise awareness. However, awareness isn't enough. To effect true, lasting change in our communities, it requires action.

The contributing authors of the *Bullyproof* series are committed to bettering their hometowns through community involvement. Many are on speaking tours, school visits, or hold bullyproof classes. They are known as the Bully Experts in their town, the go-to source of real transformation in people.

The truth is that one can't read a book, or take one workshop, or attend one pep rally and become bullyproof. It takes time, effort, energy and commitment.

These contributing authors have missions in their businesses to help kids and adults become empowered, and the best way for them is to establish an ongoing working relationship with their clients and communities.

If you, like them, are completely committed to transforming your community and making it bullyproof, and you would like to be involved in a future volume of the *Bullyproof: Unleash the Hero Inside Your Kid* series, then we should talk.

Contact Alex at www.alexchangho.com or via email at alex@alexchangho.com and let's make a difference in our communities *together.*

52609112R00076

Made in the USA
Columbia, SC
08 March 2019